THE DREAM AND THE LIE

BY SHARRAN C. TAYLOR

A.K.A. KWEEN YAKINI

Books by Author Sharran C. Taylor

Woke: A Poetic Journey

Ode To The Punani: Sensual Rising

The Dream And The Lie

Tracing Black Music To The Roots

Telling Our Blues With Black American Poetry

Website: Hookedonpoetry.com

Copyright © 2021

Original Work by Sharran C. Taylor

ISBN: 978-1-7323710-6-4

This book is a work of fiction. The names, characters, places, and incidents are products of the writer's imagination or have been used fictitiously and are not to be constructed as real. Any resemblance to persons, living or deceased, actual events, locales, or organizations is entirely coincidental.

ALL RIGHTS RESERVED

No part of this book may be reproduced, scanned, or distributed in any manner whatsoever without written permission from the author except in the case of brief quotation embodied in critical articles and reviews

AUTHOR'S NOTE

Why I Needed To Write This Book

Allow me to quote the great Toni Morrison who once said, "If there's a book that you want to read, but it has not been written yet, then you must write it." I can honestly say that has been the case for every book that I've published. Writing this collection has been a profound experience for me, and it has given me a sense of strength. My greatest hope is that after reading these poems, readers will walk away with a sense of clarity, resilience and determination.

DEDICATION

I'm dedicating this book to the ancestors who bared the blunt of this countries hatred and brutality while still showing us how to walk with dignity and pride. Right now, I am grateful to share even a little of their courage, resilience, tenacity, and determination. I sincerely want to thank them for paving the way for the generations of today, tomorrow, and beyond.

INTRODUCTION

THE DREAM AND THE LIE is a collection of poetry **that** needs to be heard! These poems were written for the purpose of enlightening minds and forcing us to have real conversations about our tragic American past. This book is a poetic storytelling of Black American history and the struggles that have followed us into America's present and, possibly, our future if we don't find a solid resolution. This book is meant to discuss the hidden traumas that were enforced upon Black Americans and the consequences of those actions. This compilation reaffirms what black folks know to be true, and that is that despite how peaceful and self-sufficient we strive to become, we've never been seen or treated as equals in this country. Undoubtedly, Black Americans have been the most hard working, innovators, and the cultural content creators in this nation's history, yet we are also the most targeted, racially profiled, incarcerated and oppressed population in America. The heart of the matter is this, Black people have never been the threatening aggressors that everyone has been taught. In fact, we are not the robbers and takers; we are the stolen treasures.

My goal for this book is to help all Americans see that Race is a made up construct that was created for the purpose of keeping white and Black people separated. This means that Black people will have to work twice as hard to achieve a fraction of their dreams while White Americans continue to live comfortably with the lie

TABLE OF CONTENTS

NOTHING ELSE BUT BLACK	*3*
IT'S TIME FOR AMERICA TO CHANGE	*10*
TO PROTECT AND SERVE	*17*
THAT OLD DEBATE	*22*
BLACK AMERICA	*31*
THAT WHITE COAT SYNDROME	*39*
THEY'RE WOKE	*48*
A LETTER FROM THE STREETS	*54*
OUR HANDS	*60*
WE ARE THE SEEDS	*65*

NOTHING ELSE BUT BLACK

NOTHING ELSE BUT BLACK

Who do you think taught you that?
I said, "Who do you think taught you that?"
And who do you think made you feel like
Life would be so much better if you weren't so Black?
Like your Blackness is somehow too Black?
Man, I can't even fathom that!

So, allow me to give you folks a quick recap
Listen, I don't know about you
But I'm sick and tired of all that!
That's why you gotta stay woke
Or else you'll keep falling for the trap!
Always keep your mind sharp
Don't get too comfortable and too lax!

Remember the sound of the whip?
And the sting of the lash?
When we did what we had to do
To keep our skin intact
And they still haven't told us
Where our forty acres is at
You see, they were born with a silver spoon

While we had to learned to adapt!
But all that being said
I still wouldn't wanna be nothing else but Black
And as a matter of fact
I wanna be Blackitty Black!
Like the way I wish Malcom could come back
And give me a "power to the people" dap!

'Cause I know, without a shadow of a doubt,
That it's a beautiful thing to be Black!
So, who made you wanna bleach your skin?
Can't you see that our melanin is under attack?

They're bewildered because our hair defies gravity
And our skin glows in the sun like it's lit
Yeah, they fear what they don't understand
That's why we were separated
When we came off those slave ships
'Cause they knew that the balance of power,
Would quickly shift!

And we know that Black civilization,
Was the beginning of everything!
That's why we were born with the birthright
Of African queens and kings

And you can feel the power in our vernacular
When "We Lift Every Voice And Sing"!
For if it weren't for Black voices,
America would have never realized
The dream of Dr. King

Listen, I'm not saying
That being Black isn't hard
But, I know in my spirit
That it's a gift from God
That's why them folks are
Trying to get a Black card!

But all kidding aside
History tells us that the original people
Were Regal and Black
So, you need to put your crown on family
And push your shoulders back!
Listen, I don't know where ya'll fell off
But I came here to get you on track !

The truth is, they wanted to erase our history
So that our culture couldn't be found
They wanted to discard our ethnic principles
Along with the inheritance of our crowns

They told us Africans were uncivilized
And that was a lie, truth be told
But they didn't tell you about King Mansa Musa,
An African so rich, he gave away bags of gold

They didn't tell you about Frederick Douglass
Who once was a slave
But who was also determined to read
Or Madam C. J. Walker
A poor black girl who became a millionaire
Who had the mind and will to succeed

You see, greatness is in our blood
'Cause we come from a different type of breed
All we have to do is open our third eye
And the universe will supply all of our needs

So, we must praise and honor our ancestors
Who courageously fought for Black pride
And we can let them other folks know
That we ain't never gone stop protesting
For saving Black lives!

And no matter what cynics may say
We know it's a blessing to be born Black

That's why they're always trying to hide the truth
You know they're afraid of how we're gonna act?

So, once you know the history and root,
You'll understand the greatness of being Black
And we have to pass down this knowledge
So that we can all have the facts!

Let others know about the excellence
Of "Black Wall Street"
And brag about our sisters
Like Rosa Parks
Who refused to give up their seats!

And we should always appreciate Black writers
Who spend their lives slaying that Black ink
So that we can all have Black books
That inspire us to think!

This means that by any means necessary,
It's up to us to keep our legacies intact
And for us to realize that we are more than worthy
Because we're the noble descendants
Of Africa to be exact!

So, before I drop this mic,
Let me give you folks this one last fact
If tomorrow was my last day on this earth,
And then the Creator decided to send me back,
My word is my bond, I wouldn't wanna be
Nothing else but Black!

IT'S TIME FOR AMERICA TO CHANGE

IT'S TIME FOR AMERICA TO CHANGE

One Mississippi
Two Mississippi
Three Mississippi
Four Mississippi
And five!

In just five seconds,
Can you fathom the number of Black folks
That have already died?
Don't bother to calculate it
Because the number is way too high

Yet y'all think it's okay to turn a blind eye
Until it's your mama that's on the news
Crying and asking "Why?"

Police brutality has been normalized!
And young people are dying way before their time!
Can't you see that these unjustified killings
Are getting way out of line?

It's getting hard to turn on the news
'Cause Black folks are dropping like flies
Living life this way should be a national crime!
So, the question is, "America,
How many more innocents have to die?"

Tell me, what will it take
For America to change?
Racism has been ignored for generations
But this country doesn't seem to be ashamed

So, Brothers and Sisters, we have to do more than march
To gain our natural-born civil rights
We have to change people's hearts and minds
If we're going to win this fight!

I know that Black folks are tired
We're tired of seeing the blood splatter
We don't wanna plan another funeral
Just so we can grieve and gather

That's why it's not enough just to say
That "Black Lives Matter"!
It's time for all Americans to change
Let's be real and stop this fake chitter-chatter

Black folks are in serious danger
We're dying in higher numbers every day
It's happening on the East Coast
It's happening on the West Coast
And, sometimes, it happens in Hampton Roads, VA

It's so heartbreaking to see mothers
Tragically forced to bury their seeds
Seems like every night on the news
We are watching our children bleed

I heard the news say a young man was killed last night
And that he was gonna be the next all-star MVP
They said a young woman was killed last week
And she was working on earning her degree
As usual, social media says "R.I.P."

So, let's get down to the real nitty gritty
'Cause some of these cops are running amuck
Like it's the wild, wild west in our cities

Black citizens are the main target
The police take us out with no pity
Brutality goes viral on our cellphones
While politicians sit in their office looking pretty

But when we protest to save Black lives
I hear complaints about some stolen loot
But all I hear are crickets
When Black folks say "Please don't shoot"

Believe me, Black folks know the deal
We know exactly what to do!
If we get pulled over by the cops
We keep our hands on the wheel
And we don't make a move!

But being born with a bullseye on our backs
Makes it easier for the police to shoot
Which makes me wonder why
Melanated skin isn't bulletproof!

We all want to see our children grow up
But it's hard for them to make long term plans
If a cellphone seems to looks like
They have a gun in their hands

Listen, Black children are endangered
I see them dying way too fast
Cops say they had no choice
Then they turn around and laugh

So, this trauma is all too common here
On these streets, Black folks just disappear
We keep losing our people to violence and fear
We die in higher numbers year after year

And that's why the police
Have lost our respect
They act like they forgot
Who they are getting paid to protect

We see their hands in their pockets
While they kneel down on our necks
They find our babies hanging from trees
And they haven't found one suspect yet!

They write laws that allow them
To shoot us in our homes and in our backs
I hear them make up excuses like
They were mysteriously triggered to react

So, even if we're having a good ol' time
Grilling with the fam on a lovely day
If white folks make one phone call
The cops show up looking like
They wanna kill a Black man today

Then we go right back to...

One Mississippi
Two Mississippi
Three Mississippi
Four Mississippi
And five!

In just five seconds,
Can you fathom the number of Black folks
That have already died?
Don't bother to calculate it
Because the number is way too high

Yet y'all still think it's okay to turn a blind eye
Until it's your mama that's on the news
Crying and asking "Why?"

TO PROTECT AND SERVE

TO PROTECT AND SERVE

What's that you said?
To protect and serve?
Wow, I can't believe what I just heard!
Oh, I know who the slave patrol
Are meant to protect and serve
So, until racism is dismantled
That sounds like some foolish blurb

Black folks look at your actions!
We're not swayed by your words
American history tells a different story
So, you really sound absurd!

Listen, in these here United States
Police brutality happens right in front of our face
'Cause when it comes to killing Black folks
These cops don't hesitate!

This country has no justified alibi
Look, these killings are being recorded live!
Politically analyzed and then normalized
The DOJ acts like they are legally blind
So no, Black folks ain't the least bit surprised!

But now cops are complaining
About being too harshly criticized
When it's clear that they do more to protect each other
Then they do to protect Black lives!

The truth is that these injustices are institutionalized
And that is an indisputable fact
So, no matter how free America claims we are,
When it comes to Black folks, the police overreact

We're always the primary suspects
And it doesn't matter how educated we are
Or how compliant we seem to act
The statistics are reporting the truth,
Which is that Black bodies are under attack!

If you know the real American history
You'll understand why we are in this current state
It's because the police used to be the slave patrol
So, they were created to capture the enslaved

Those who grew up in the South already know
That going hunting for runaways was a pastime goal
They love torturing those who tried to escape
Before taking them back to their masters' home

So, what we are seeing today
Is just our history being shown
And this ain't new to Black folks
For us, this has a very familiar tone!

Although their methods have changed
We can see the mindset has stayed the same
They stopped wearing white hoods
Yeah, that's all well and good
And the KKK even changed their name

But they still have legal protection
They also have a "blue wall of silence"
So, they don't have to tell their superiors
About any misconduct or unethical violence

You keep saying that things are different
And that slavery happened so long ago
But if they're not protecting Black folks
Seems like we're still living under Jim Crow

You can't believe that we're free
When the cops can strangle us until we sleep
Or kneel down on our windpipe
And choke us with one knee

They say we resisted and we tried to put up a fight
When they don't even read us our Miranda rights
But in America this is what street justice looks like
Listen, you can't even begin to understand our plight!

The police no-knock warrants that allow them
To enter our homes with shotguns or pistols
Then the DOJ will offer them immunity
And granted quick dismissals

So, tell me whose here to protect and serve?
Wow, I can't believe what I just heard!
Listen, we know about the slave patrol
And who they were meant to protect and serve
So, until racism is dismantled
That sounds like a foolish blurb
Cause' we look at your actions!
We're not swayed by your words
American history tells a different story
So, you really sound absurd!

THAT OLD DEBATE

THAT OLD DEBATE

Excuse me, but were y'all just saying?
That America is fading
Because the other groups are invading?
And now white Americans are complaining
That their power is draining
So, making America great again
Is what you've been hypocritically debating?

Well, for goodness sake!
Please, give us a break
With all that talk about making America great!
Stop spreading the lies and hate
Unless you're prepared to elaborate
'Cause it's nonsensical to say that America was great
When the white majority use to dominate
I know y'all can't be seriously having that old debate
But believe me, I have no problem
With setting that record straight!

Listen, America wasn't great
When we did all the cooking and cleaning
And our lives were stripped of meaning

No, it wasn't great when we were the help
And white folks acquired all the wealth
Or when they sat at the table and ate
While we waited to put food on their plates
But then, I guess you would think that
Those time were great
I bet those are the moments
That you'd like to commemorate
But Black folks didn't think it was great
When you didn't consider
Us to be members of the human race
Or when y'all paraded around
Looking like fools in Blackface
Telling jokes about all the
Watermelon and fried chicken we ate

No, America wasn't great
That's why we had to force the
School system to integrate
So that our children wouldn't be
Indoctrinated with hate
And so their minds would elevate
But hold up, wait!
If America was so great,
Then what happened to your honor?

Why don't you feel ashamed
About how your ancestors took pleasure
In brutalizing the enslaved?
So, tell us how America was great?
'Cause what we still remember
Is all the racism and hate
That us Black folks had to tolerate

And it sure wasn't great
When white folks were celebrating
About the nooses they were making
They smiled just thinking
About all the lynchings
And the sounds of
Tree branches breaking
From the torturing
Or the savage raping
Which, tragically for us,
There was no escaping
So, we just kept on waiting
For our emancipation
On them old and evil plantations
And it was hell for us
But I guess for y'all
It must have seemed like a vacation

Yeah, we remember when Americans
Had them angry white mobs
And them white folks felt powerful and hyped
Today, Black men become target practice for the police
If they get caught outside too late at night

And instead of that old plantation
Now they give us incarceration
They make us work for free
While they receive compensation
It's the same old same system
Just a different situation

And do you think America was great for us?
When we were picking that cotton
Maybe y'all don't remember
But we haven't forgotten
How you showed us no mercy
Back then, y'all souls were rotten

That's why I couldn't believe
When I heard you saying
That America is fading
Because the other groups are invading
And now white folks are complaining

That their power is draining
So, making America great again
Is what you're hypocritically debating?

Yeah, that's when I knew
That you needed a clue
And that it was time for me to enlighten you
About the importance of Black institutions
And how Black folks have been fighting
To amend America's constitution
'Cause we've always been productive citizens
For centuries, we've been providing solutions
So, how can you be so disrespectful
And seek retribution?
When we've made countless contributions!

Maybe it's because Black history
Has often been overlooked
And omitted from your, "High Academic" study books

So, you may not know that
Black folks are great innovators
And educators
Yeah, we invented
Door elevators

Engine generators
And refrigerators
So, how can you be a discriminator?

When there are far too many inventions
For me to mention
We even invented
Medicine, math and the alphabet
So, now do I have your attention?

Listen, don't you think it's about time
That Black folks were truly appreciated
For the country that we've cultivated!

Yes, together we've created
A distinctive melting pot
After all, America is the home
Of jazz, R&B, and hip hop
Our musicians are the bomb!
Don't act like you forgot

Listen, Black people have done a lot
And, truth be told, it doesn't matter
If you like us or not
But you couldn't possibly try to lecture me

About Americas' true history
Or about how great you think America used to be
Why don't you try reading some Black books
To help you really see!

Yes, I could go on for days!
About the value of Black people
And what we deserve to be paid
While you're still pathetically dreaming
About those dark and perilous days
But I think you've got the message
And I know my point has been made
So, I guess I'll go home
And cool in the shade
Have me a glass of wine
Or maybe a glass of lemonade

But please stop talking about America is fading
'Cause we've only just begun
And the privileged shouldn't have all the power
We must learn to share and live as one
So, can you just give us a break?
With that talk about making America great
It's time to stop spreading the lies and hate
When, clearly, you're unable to elaborate

About how America was so great
When the white majority used to dominate
There is no way y'all could possibly win
That old debate
But believe me, I have no problem
With setting that record straight!

BLACK AMERICA

BLACK AMERICA

Welcome to Black America!
You'd better recognize where you stand
Learn the real history
Because we've poured a lot of blood on this land

And don't be so quick to believe
Everything you see on American T.V.
Because here in Black America,
We have a different reality!

Yes, we've built the "White House"
And just about everything else you see
But because of idea of White Supremacy
We're still fighting for our justice and liberty

In Black America, history is being whitewashed
They try to diminish our self-worth and dignity
Here, civil rights are never equal
And they allow the police to go on killing sprees

American, poverty is a condition
That has constantly been ignored and denied

Truthfully, for Black Americans,
Most of us will remain economically poor
Until the day we die

Despite the fact that we are citizens,
They still don't want us to be free
I know that sounds strange
So, let me explain
Before you fly over our shining seas

Immigrants believe that America is the place
Where they can be free
And their problems will dissipate
But Black Americans have lived with the
Brutality, injustice and hate
So, ain't no way this country will ever be great

We have faced many challenges
We've survived despite the oppression and disrespect
The police keep on killing our brothers and sisters
That's why you see so much chaos and civil unrest

But we can always count on our politicians
To lie to the voters that they neglect
So, Black folks always keep a side hustle

To make a percentage of what the white folks' get

This country loves to celebrate
They have cookouts for Labor Day
Yet it ignores reparations for Black folks
They took our land but we ain't never been paid

Let me paraphrase Fredrick Douglass
"What is the Fourth of July to a slave?"
But thank the all mighty for Juneteenth
That's our official Freedom Day

For years they have tried to indoctrinate us
To believe in their ridiculous Columbus Day
When they rejoice about a confused man
Who simply lost his way

Oh, and they love to commemorate Thanksgiving
While ignoring the slaughter of Indigenous Americans
Who were settled here and peacefully living

But if we look back in American History
We will acknowledge the Emancipation Proclamation
When we were promised forty acres and a mule
Until the day of Lincoln's assassination

Believe me, this left Black folks
In a dire situation
'Cause after 246 years of slavery,
We wanted some economic fortification

But instead, what we got
Were lynchings and assassinations
Even in the 20th century
They don't think we deserve our reparations!

Now, if you still don't understand Black America,
Maybe you need a few examples
America is far from perfect
Allow me to give you just a few samples

In 1919 America had "The Red Summer"
When White folks were lynching
Black families nationwide
Forcing us to leave our homes in a panic
Running in fear for our lives

In 1906 we created a place called "Black Wall Street"
Which became a very successful Black town
Where Black folks came to conduct their business
From miles and miles around

But White folks in Tulsa couldn't stand to see
Black folks feeling empowered in their town
So, they told a white lie in order to justify
Killing innocent people and burning it down

This event became known as the Greenwood massacre
It was in 1921 when White mobs went on the attack
They bombed a prosperous Black community
They destroyed everything that pertained to Blacks

After fighting for so many decades
We still didn't have real peace
So, we marched with Dr. King
Black folks stood ten toes down in the streets

We called it the Civil Rights Movement
By any means necessary, we wanted a change
We fought real hard against oppression
It must have been the blood of Nat Turner
Running through our veins

Then we saw the dream of Martin
We raised one fist and walked over mountains
Till we became bold enough to
Drink water from their whites only fountains

We became steadfast like Rosa Parks
Who said, "No, I will not be moved"
Listen, Black people are true citizens of this land
And we'll keep fighting to have the same rights as you

We are also warriors like Malcolm
Who walked his path with no fear in his eyes
And we are strong like his widow, Betty Shabazz,
Who was able to keep her family going
After her king had died

We are justified like Angela Davis
Who demanded our equal rights
And we are fearless like Muhamad Ali
Who told them white folks
That he refused to fight!

Yes, we've had many great leaders
Who've devoted their lives to keeping us free
And we have many intellectual writers
Who will continue to document our legacies

But, even today, some white folks still call the cops
If they see a Black civilian in their exclusive neighborhoods
Then the cops will stop and ask us if we're lost

Because Black folks ain't supposed to live that good

And after everything we've endured
We don't understand how they can still see us as a threat
Black folks have been given the worse possible hand
Yet white folks still have the nerve to be upset

So, that's how it remains in Black America
And you must recognize where you stand
Take the time to learn the real history
'Cause we have shed a lot of blood on this land

And don't be so quick to believe
Everything you see on American T.V.
'Cause here in Black America,
We have a different reality!

Yes, we did build the "White House"
And just about everything else you see
But because of idea of White Supremacy
We're still fighting for our justice and liberty

THAT WHITE COAT SYNDROME

WHY BLACK FOLKS HAVE A DISTRUST OF THE MEDICAL SYSTEM

We know that slavery lasted for 246 years in America, but after it ended, Black folks were still seen as subhuman. Thus, the mentality of racism still existed in American society for many years to come, and Black folks would endure some of the most inhumane treatments known to any medical patient. It is a fact that doctors were heavily swayed by a belief system of superiority, which was clearly demonstrated in their approach to treating Black people. Thus, they did not treat us like their average white patients. On the contrary, they treated Black folks like test subjects they used without Black folks' consent or knowledge. To be blunt, they were sometimes using Black folks to create biological and chemical weapons. Many of the so-called "treatments" they performed on Black people would be considered torture today. It has been documented that doctors were also known to perform tests on some military personnel by deliberately exposing them to infectious agents. One example of this would be the "Tuskegee Institute." They told a group of 600 Black men who were infected with syphilis that they were being treated for "bad blood." As a result of many deceptive practices, a high level of distrust began to form. In addition, it can be said that it's not a coincidence that Black folks have had the worst health care, the worst health status, and the worst health outcome of any race or ethnic group in U.S. history. Yes, we all need and want doctors that we can trust, but for Black folks, we will always have more questions when it comes to choosing a doctor, if we decide to seek care at all.

WHAT IS THAT WHITE COAT SYNDROME?

The white coat syndrome is a natural distrust and fear towards doctors and/or white coats that has developed over generations in the Black community. This phenomenon occurred as the result of years of unethical and malicious malpractice on the part of white doctors that were allowed to go on for centuries in America. Because so many atrocities have been perpetrated, I would say that it would be unnatural for Black people to not have some fear of the medical community.

THAT WHITE COAT SYNDROME

Hey, I think I've got that white coat syndrome!
I've heard it's a hereditary affliction
Maybe I got it from my grandmother
I bet a lot of Black folks have found themselves
In this same fatal position!

But I don't want no fake maltreatment
That's only meant to pull me in as a lure
I wanna find me a holistic doctor
Whose intentions are heartfelt and pure
A doctor who knows the right herbs
One who will nurture and reassure
I wanna find me a Dr. Sebi
Who will actually give me the cure!

And Grandma said, "If you go to a doctor,
Then you better be careful about the one you pick"
So, I'm gonna ask for references
The same way I would check out a mechanic
Before I give them my car to fix

But if I'm really feeling sick

I want a doctor that's legit!
And I want a trusted doctor
That we all know
Not some mad scientist who wants to inject me
With some phony placebo!

Grandma said, "Don't go near those twisted physicians
Who'll leave your body in a chronic condition
So, they can shorten your life span
By giving you some bogus prescription"

She once told me about this so-called doctor
America named him the "father of gynecology"
They praised him for his medical contributions
Despite his racist ideology

He callously performed genital surgery
On Black women who were enslaved
And he didn't give them anesthesia
'Cause he believed that Black people couldn't feel pain
Yet, America showed no remorse
In fact, they built a statue to honor his name

So, they ain't gonna be using me
For some new risky operation

Or any kind of medical exploitation
'Cause I heard all about how they used us
In those unethical experimentations

Like when those drug companies ran test trials of AZT
On African women infected with HIV
They said, "Come to our clinic
And we'll give you those treatments for free"

Yeah, those slick pharmaceutical corporations
They love to use folks from African nations
They offer their patients prime medication
But the results are just more healthcare violations

Those doctors never gave them the real thing
'Cause they were just doing research
To learn what symptoms the disease would bring

So, Black folks shared their experiences
Of the abuse they endured back then
They said white doctors didn't treat them well
If they weren't family, friend, or some kind of kin

That's why folks don't wanna go to the hospital
Because of all the deceit and the lies

Old folks say, "Once you go in,
You might not make it out alive!"

America has even acknowledged
And confirmed our worst fears
That Black folks have been doctors' lab rats
And guinea pigs for hundreds of years

They admitted giving hepatitis to mental patients
And issuing lethal dosages at will
They infected healthy people with the flu
And injected cancer cells into the chronically ill

They've experimented on helpless children
And our mentally incapacitated
As they've done with our needy, our uneducated,
And them poor Black folks they have incarcerated

But, here in America,
This is the dilemma we face
Even when it's time to call 911
Some of us will still hesitate
Until our bodies are so weak
That they say it might be too late

So, we end up in the ER
Going into cardiac arrest
We hear them paging "code blue"
As they beat on our chest

And we can't afford their medications
They say the brand names work the best
So, we settle for generic remedies
And we hope it's not some kind of test

So, when they tell us about some new virus
A lot of us still don't trust those doctors or chemists
They tell us we need to take a new vaccine
But old folks remember when a lot of doctors
Were racist academics

Historically we don't trust doctors
Who didn't care about our suffering and pain
We've learned if you don't go to the right one
Your good health may be in vain

We know that white folks are living longer
While Black folks remain in poor health
Medicine and food cost is too high for us
Whereas they come from families

With generational wealth

But maybe I've got that white coat syndrome!
I've heard it's a hereditary affliction
Maybe I got it from my grandmother
I bet a lot of Black folks have found themselves
In this same fatal position!

But I don't want no fake maltreatment
That's only meant to pull me in as a lure
I wanna find me a holistic doctor
Whose intentions are heartfelt and pure
A doctor who knows the right herbs
One who will nurture and reassure
I wanna find me a Dr. Sebi
Who will actually give me the cure!

THEY'RE WOKE

THEY'RE WOKE

Hey, you better listen to me folks!
'Cause I'm telling you those Black folks are woke!
Can't you feel the ground breaking?
This is gonna be epic and earthshaking!
They're about to judge us
Like the book of Revelation!
They're gonna burn down those prison plantations!
So, I want the government
To perform a full investigation!
'Cause those folks are woke!

Hey, do you think we're gonna need some more rope?
How many more Black leaders are we gonna have to choke?
Somebody better come up with a bogus quote
'Cause I need to know, how we're gonna steal their votes?
But first, I wanna know
Who's waking up these folks?
Is it the media or the school systems?
Hell no!

Hey, did you hear what I said?

Tell the police it's about to be a "code red"
Or maybe it's a "code blue"
Look, I don't know what these folks
Are about to do!

Listen, go and get my protector's son!
Go tell the NRA
That we're gonna need more guns
'Cause we're about to have a Black rebellion
I think it's too late to call 9-1-1

So, I think we should take a moment of silence
I know this Civil rights movement is gonna be terrifying
Oh my God, these folks just might triumph
And become even more defiant and less compliant
Because somebody done woke these sleeping giants

Oh, God! I'm beginning to feel threatened
'Cause these blind sheep
Have now become the new weapon
I'm telling you this will be Armageddon
We're gonna have a lot of souls
Praying for Heaven

Maybe we should call the FBI

Or some vigilante caped crusaders
'Cause I think these folks
Are about to give us our walking papers
I think we're about to catch the vapors
I heard they're calling us the traitors
They're saying we're the haters
And I think they might be packing
Some kind of lightsabers!

Please tell me how we're gon' appease these folks
No, we can't just stand by and do nothing
While they become woke
'Cause then they might start to have
A little too much hope
And become too easily provoked
We gon' need a miracle soon
So, maybe we should call the pope!

'Cause they're saying that America ain't right
I heard they told the president to go take a hike
And I have never seen these Black voters so hyped
I think they're finally starting to see the light!

Can't you see that these folks are awake
It's time to call the National Guard for goodness sake!

Because it's our white privilege that's really at stake!
We gave them too much freedom
Maybe that was our biggest mistake
But now it feels like this country is heading
For a constitutional break
And our time might be done
Like icing on the proverbial cake!

They got access to too much information
They're posting too much on social media
And now they're using Google
To get to Wikipedia?

They're researching our lies
They're learning the truth
Listen, I'm trying to tell you
I think they've found the proof

Listen, this could be the new terrorism!
'Cause they'll have more skepticism
About our fake journalism
And they might wanna redefine patriotism
So, they can do away with systemic racism

So, you'd better listen up, folks!

'Cause I'm telling you those folks are woke!

Can't you feel the ground breaking?

This is gonna be epic and earthshaking!

They're about to judge us

Like the book of Revelation!

They're gonna burn down those prison plantations!

So, I want the government

To perform a full investigation!

'Cause those Blacks folks are woke!

A LETTER FROM THE STREETS

A LETTER FROM THE STREETS

Dear Loved Ones,
The Streets would like to say, "Thank you"
Thank you for all the Keeshas and Hakeems
Especially the ones about ages ten through seventeen
Thank you for letting them linger in our streets
'Cause it only takes one small beef
Before someone calls the police
Too bad they weren't as smart as they seemed
But now they're just another statistic
Body outlined in chalk at homicide scenes

We have no sympathy or have time for excuses
We're not concerned about your child being bored
So, here's a little tip: try building their ambitions
And it wouldn't hurt to give them more house chores
We advise you to heed this warning
And do what you must to keep those children indoors

'Cause it's not our policy to nurture or protect
My, what a tragedy, you've only got one left
I think the last one was killed in a drive-by
And your absence was the cause of death

Now they're in the hands of The Streets
About to take their very last breath

You see, the streets are filled with
Large egos that want to be stroked
And murderers just waiting to be provoked
With disagreeable conversations
Fueled by heated escalations
Which are likely to end with physical confrontations
That may lead to some type of criminalization
Followed by a lengthy incarceration
So that they can become ex-cons
Who will probably commit parole violations.
Which can give the judge a solid justification
To dismiss an early release
But offer an early extermination

So, be sure to keep them in a child's place
And stop letting them think they're grown
They're really too young and naive
To have a complete mind of their own

Please believe us, Loved Ones, we are The Streets
Although we have no moral obligations,
We can generously offer your children

Hospitalizations from brutal initiations
As well as a steady decline of motivation
With occasional suicide contemplations
So, we would truly like to thank you
For your unwilling donations

'Cause it's not our responsibility
To watch or protect them
We don't share your warm sentiment
Since it's our job to neglect them

And these children are so easily agitated
So disrespectful and mean
With plenty of luck, a small percentage
Might even live to be nineteen
They can grow up to be the next predators
With a chip on their shoulder and a lack of dreams
We promise the ending will not be good
If they end up playing for our team

Yes, we love to see our children
Gang banging and drug slanging
It won't be too long
Before we hear church organs and praying

Listen, you can't blame us for the lives that they gave
Because the streets accept anyone who enlist
Even if they're barely old enough to shave
We shower them with weapons
We make it easy to release all that rage
We always give them choices
It's either prison or the grave
Because we are the streets!
And it's not our job to spare souls
Who don't want to be saved!

Dear Moms and Dads,
We understand how hard it is
For you to go to work
And then come home to raise your kids
So, just leave that job to us
And we'll make sure they don't live

So, let us end with, "Ashes to ashes and dust to dust"
It's so nice doing business with you
And, in your children, we continue to trust

Remember, we'll keep doing our part
And may their young souls rest in peace
But now, we're looking for some fresh recruits

Sincerely, Signed: The Streets!

OUR HANDS

OUR HANDS

Dear God, we thank you for giving us hands
We are so blessed to have hands to embrace
And to give hugs with
Especially for giving us quick hands
That we can swat away unwanted bugs with

And thank you for giving us hands
That can plant seeds and help them grow
We're thankful for playful hands
That can make balls out of the fluffy snow

Thank you for construction hands that can build homes
And ones that can lay all those heavy bricks
Thank you for handy hands around the house
When we need to have something fixed

We're thankful for culinary hands that cook
And hands that know how to hunt and fish
Thank you for giving us hands to build campfires
And hands that gather up wood and sticks

We thank you for artistic hands

And for fingers that can snap with applauds
Yes, we're very thankful that we have two hands
When we need to pull up our sagging draws

We're thankful for hands to write love notes
'Cause they can really touch our hearts
And we're thankful we've hands to vote
So, that we can do our part!

We welcome friendly hands that wave "hello"
And we mourn the hands that say "goodbye"
We're grateful for gentle hands
To wipe the tears away from our eyes

Thank you for teaching hands to write lessons
And for smart hands to help us with our taxes
Thankful for hands to fold laundry
And for the ones that fix our broken glasses

We respect those firm handshakes
When business meetings are complete
And we appreciate an extended hand
Offered as a gesture of goodwill and peace

But, today, I heard the police yelling at this man

They said:
"Turn around! Don't move! Stop where you stand!"
I watched the scene in horror
As he slowly raised his hands
They had their weapons aimed and ready
Without even knowing if he was a guilty man

I yelled, "He's done what you asked
So, you have no reason to shoot!
He wants to show you that he's innocent
But you won't let him give you the proof"

And I couldn't take my eyes off of his hands
Because I know they've done so much
But the police couldn't see his greatness
All they wanted to see were his hands in cuffs

I'll never forget the look on his face
As they tackled him and dragged him away
I said, "God, please watch over him
For this might be the end of his days"

They drove him down to their station
Where they defiled his hands with ink
Now every time he looks down at his hands

That tragic moment will always make him think

Because no matter how much he has contributed
With using the gift of his God-given hands,
Society will never truly understand
The value of a Black Man's hands!

WE ARE THE SEEDS

WE ARE THE SEEDS

We carry the blood of our ancestors
We are the seeds that were sown on plantations
There is a natural resistance within our blood
Because we are the descendants of past generations

Though our enemies may sit and wonder
With heavy thoughts and contemplation
About why we were born with this level of strength
And unwavering determination

They are afraid to acknowledge
That we are an essential population!
And that we were chosen to be present in this world
For we are the seeds of the African nations!

History tells us how cruel the white colonizers were
And that they had a hunger for African importations
They captured our men, women, and children
And the world profited for countless generations

They used many inhumane methods
To secure our captivity and subjugation

And never before had there ever been
Such a deliberate and prolonged annihilation
Yet we still survived a horrific trauma
Because we fought for our own emancipation

We lost so many souls fighting for freedom
And removing the whips from our backs
We fought against the desecration of our dignity
That was constantly under attack!

And even when our spirits had withered
They kept our families divided
Because they feared that our warrior spirits
Would rise up and become defiant

They knew we had a God like spirit
That made us strong and brave
And no matter what they did to us
We were never meant to be slaves

Black people have never been weak
Even when they tried to mock us with doubt
We were always meant to survive
Because that's what our DNA is all about

Yes our roots are solid and unshakeable
Our bond with the Ancestors is unbreakable
Our existence is vital and unmistakable
When we unite we are more than capable

We are stronger than they can ever fathom
We are the earth beneath the tree
We're the Black seeds from the harvest
We don't understand the meaning of defeat

Yes, we've endured much pain and sorrow
But we will never be destroyed
That's why our enemies keep watching us
They seem to be quite angry and annoyed

They ponder with great frustration
How we've still managed to survive
Although they've used every weapon against us,
We stand here beaming with confidence and pride

Naturally, we carry the blood of our ancestors
We are the seeds that were sown on plantations
There is a natural resistance within our blood
Because we are the descendants of past generations!

So, our enemies may still sit and wonder
With heavy thoughts and contemplation
About why we were born with this level of strength
And unwavering determination

They are afraid to acknowledge
That we are an essential population!
And that we were chosen to be present in this world
For we are the seeds of the African nations!

Thank you for reading

THE DREAM AND THE LIE

You can leave the author a book review on Amazon.com

Go to: amazon.com/author/sharrantaylor

Website: HookedOnPoetry.com

Contact Email: sharranctaylor@gmail.com

Wishing You Love, Light, & Blessings!

www.ingramcontent.com/pod-product-compliance
Ingram Content Group UK Ltd.
Pitfield, Milton Keynes, MK11 3LW, UK
UKHW041424180426
11947UKWH00007B/280